PEGASUS ENCYCLOPEDIA LIBRARY

Animal World
AMPHIBIANS

Edited by: Pallabi B. Tomar, Hitesh Iplani
Managing editor: Tapasi De
Designed by: Vijesh Chahal, Anil Kumar and Rohit Kumar
Illustrated by: Suman S. Roy, Tanoy Choudhury
Colouring done by: Vinay Kumar, Kiran Kumari & Pradeep Kumar

CONTENTS

What are amphibians? 3

How amphibians evolved 4

Category of amphibians 6

Where are amphibians found? 9

Behaviour 10

Amphibian hibernation and aestivation 11

Food habits 12

Means of defence 13

Environmental significance 15

Some well-known amphibians 16

Test Your Memory 31

Index 32

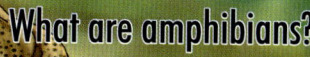

What are amphibians?

Like birds, reptiles, mammals, and fishes, amphibians are vertebrates — that is, creatures with a backbone. Amphibians live part of their life in water and part on land. The word amphibian means 'both sides of life'. This is because the amphibian begins its life in the water and then finishes it mainly on land. The change of an animal in its appearance from baby to adult is called metamorphosis. An amphibian goes through metamorphosis as it grows from a baby to an adult.

There are about 4,780 species of amphibians known, and there maybe 300 to 500 more that have yet to be discovered. Amphibians are cold-blooded; their body temperature depends on the temperature of their environment. There are three groups (orders) of living amphibians: newts and salamanders (urodeles); frogs and toads (anurans); and caecilians (the worm-like gymnophiones).

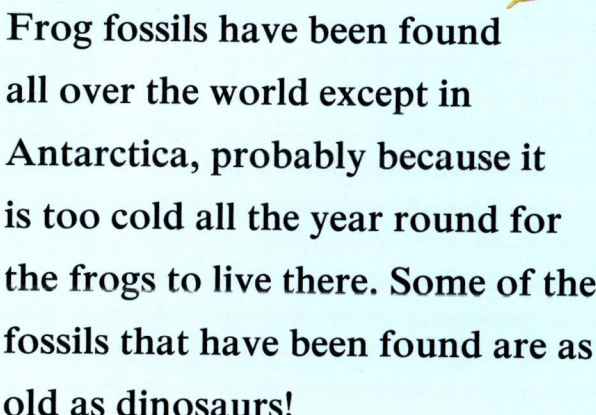

Astonishing fact

Frog fossils have been found all over the world except in Antarctica, probably because it is too cold all the year round for the frogs to live there. Some of the fossils that have been found are as old as dinosaurs!

How amphibians evolved

Amphibians evolved from fish about 400 million years ago, when the amount of dry land on Earth increased greatly. Certain fish adapted to these changing conditions by gradually developing limbs to crawl with and lungs to breathe with. Such organisms, capable of life both in water and on land, came to be called amphibians, a name that means 'double life'. Amphibians were the first vertebrates (animals with backbones) to live on land. However, they returned to the water to breed.

Characteristics

Amphibians have developed in many different ways in order to survive in areas with widely changing climates, dangers, and food sources.

Most amphibians are relatively small animals. Except for the Chinese giant salamander, the giants among them became extinct long ago. They vary in length from less than 2/5 inch to over 60 inches. The West African Goliath frog grows to more than 30 cm in length and may weigh as much as a full-grown house cat. Most of the species have four limbs. The hands generally end in four fingers and the feet in five toes. Although the limbless gymnophions crawl, most amphibians with legs move by jumping, climbing or running.

Amphibians do not chew with their teeth. They use their long, flexible tongues to capture their prey, which they then swallow whole.

Astonishing fact

More than 75 per cent of all toad and frog species in the world live in the tropical rainforests!

How amphibians evolved

The moist skin of most amphibians provides protection and absorbs water and oxygen. The upper skin layer, called the epidermis, is regularly shed in a process called moulting. The skin usually comes off in one piece and is then eaten by the animal.

The lower skin layer, called the dermis, often includes mucous and poison glands. The mucous glands help provide essential moisture to the body. The protective poison glands produce poisons that are harmful to their natural enemies, such as birds and small mammals, but that rarely harm humans.

These glandular secretions give some amphibians distinct odours. The spotted salamander and the common toad smell of vanilla. Some frogs smell of onion and the fire-bellied toad smells of garlic.

The skin's protective properties include the ability to change colour so that the animal can hide when an enemy is nearby. Sometimes parts of the skin become brightly coloured. The amphibian displays these colours to enemies to warn them to keep away.

Astonishing fact

Frog bones form a growth ring every year when the frog is hibernating. Scientists can count these rings to discover the age of the frog.

The sense organs differ greatly, depending on the order and the species. The eyes are virtually useless in underground amphibians but are well-developed in other species. The sense of smell is generally good. Hearing ability varies according to the species. Some amphibians also have pores on their bodies that are sensitive to vibrations in the water.

Category of amphibians

Anurans

Frogs and toads make up the order Anura, the largest group of living amphibians, comprising about 3,000 species. Anurans lack tails and have long hind legs that are well adapted for jumping and swimming. Most anurans live in areas where there is fresh water, although some are well adapted to drier habitats.

Astonishing fact

People who study amphibians are called herpetologists.

It will take three years before the froglet will reach maturity and the cycle starts all over again!

In early spring, the male frog arrives at the pond and may have travelled up to one mile to get there! He attracts the female with a loud croaking sound.

At twelve to fourteen weeks the tail disappears and the tiny froglet is ready to leave the water.

The eggs or frogspawn are surrounded by jelly. A clutch of frogspawn can contain to 4,000 eggs.

Ten to eleven weeks and the front legs have also appeared.

After about 10 days a tadpole wriggles out of each egg.

After eight weeks the back legs have formed.

At first it uses its gills to breath, but after five weeks the tadpole develops lungs and has to swim to the top of the water to breath air.

Life Cycle of the Common Frog

Category of amphibians

Frogs and toads live mainly on a diet of insects and other invertebrates. The largest frogs and toads also eat small mammals, birds, fish, and other amphibians. Frogs of all kinds (including toads) make up the biggest order of amphibians with about 4,000 species around the globe.

Frogs have large eyes on the tops of their heads. Many frogs have poison glands in their skin. Most frogs and toads have distinct songs or calls that are used by males during the mating season. Frogs have short front legs and long, powerful hind legs. They have four toes on their front feet and five toes on their hind feet.

Urodeles

The order Urodela contains about 250 species of newts and salamanders. Urodeles range in size from approximately 4 inches to the largest of all amphibians, the giant salamander of Japan, which grows to more than about 1.5 m. Urodeles have long tails and small, underdeveloped legs. They are usually found in or near water and often reside in moist soil under rocks or logs. Adults usually spend most of their time on land and have a diet consisting of insects and worms.

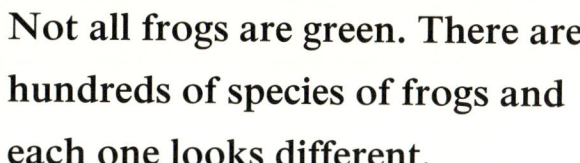

Astonishing fact

Not all frogs are green. There are hundreds of species of frogs and each one looks different.

AMPHIBIANS

Salamanders

Salamanders are not nearly as common as frogs, totalling only some 410 known species. North America, with about 150 species, is the best place in the world to see salamanders.

Salamanders have slender bodies and tails. Their legs are about equal in length. Salamander skin is moist and usually smooth. Most salamanders have four toes on the front feet and five toes on the hind feet. Salamanders are usually both 'inconspicuous' and 'nocturnal'—that is, they don't bring attention to themselves and they prefer the night time.

Astonishing fact
When attacked, Salamanders release a milky toxic chemical from their skin.

Gymnophions

Caecilians of the order Gymnophiona are blind, legless amphibians shaped like worms. They burrow in moist soil in tropical habitats of Africa and South America, feeding on soil invertebrates such as worms. There are at least 160 species of caecilians.

Caecilian

Salamander

Where are amphibians found?

The distribution of amphibians is worldwide, except in Antarctica and Greenland. They are found on landmasses and in fresh water. Frogs are the most widespread of the three groups. They live in a great variety of habitats, ranging from deserts to rain forests, permanent ponds to high mountain meadows.

Salamanders occur primarily in North America, Europe, and Asia. Salamanders occupy a variety of terrestrial and aquatic habitats; those found in dry environments, such as the Mexican plateau, usually live in ponds. When on land, they are often found in moist leaf litter and under rocks and logs. In northern areas several species are found in ponds, streams, or rivers.

The caecilians are tropical in distribution. They occur from southern Mexico to northern Argentina, in tropical Africa, and in Southeast Asia. These limbless elongate, virtually tailless animals are usually burrowers. They are found in stream banks, under debris, and along root channels from sea level to 3,000 m.

Amphibians occur widely throughout the world, even north of the Arctic Circle in Eurasia. They are absent only in Antarctica, most remote oceanic islands, and extremely dry deserts. .

Astonishing fact

The male frog is the only one, who can croak, and every frog species makes its own unique sound and some are not even croaks. Some frogs whistle and some chirp like a bird.

Behaviour

All amphibians must live near water because their soft skin provides little protection against dehydration. If their skin dries up, they soon die. Most live in the areas between fresh water and dry land or in regions that have plenty of dew and moisture.

Some species of amphibians are active by day, while others move about at night. Their activity is also influenced by temperature and humidity.

Amphibians are cold-blooded animals, meaning they are about the same temperature as their environment. When the temperature drops or rises or the humidity falls, they change habitats in order to become more comfortable.

Some amphibians are considered moderately intelligent. They are known to communicate with each other by calls or croaks that indicate mating, distress, or territorial concerns. Sounds, which vary greatly among the species, are made by the passage of air across the vocal cords. Male frogs have vocal sacs on either side of the throat. These act to amplify sounds. Some frogs and toads even sing in chorus.

Frogs and toads have a strong sense of location. When taken from their territories or breeding grounds, they can find their way back by smell and instinctively by the position of the stars. Many migratory species tend to return to the same breeding grounds year after year.

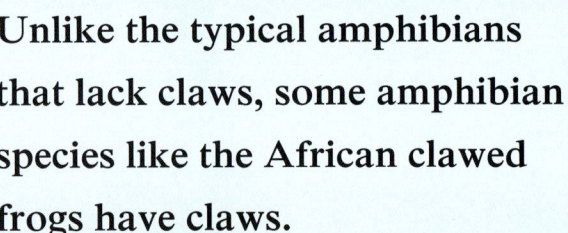

Astonishing fact

Unlike the typical amphibians that lack claws, some amphibian species like the African clawed frogs have claws.

Hibernation and aestivation

The main way amphibians deal with winter's cold temperatures is to hibernate, or to 'go dormant'. Different amphibian species hibernate in different ways.

When cold weather comes many kinds of frogs swim to the bottoms of ponds and lakes where they rest on the bottom or partially burrow into the mud. Frogs have highly specialized skin that allows them to absorb oxygen through their skin, and give off carbon dioxide the same way. Many species can survive underwater for months, their bodies very slowly burning fat stored in their bodies.

Sometimes amphibians such as toads hibernate on land, digging below the frost line to avoid freezing. Certain salamanders may also hibernate deep below the ground's surface, but they can't dig the way toads can, so they search for abandoned burrows or other natural holes.

Some frogs can actually freeze solid. When cold weather approaches they just burrow under the forest floor's leaves and debris. When freezing weather comes, much of the water in their bodies goes out, its veins fill with an antifreeze-like mixture, and then the frog simply freezes.

Hot, dry weather also can be stressful for amphibians and often during such times they may go dormant. However, now instead of being called hibernation it's called aestivation. When some amphibians aestivate they move underground where it is cooler and more humid. During aestivation an amphibian's breathing, heart rate, and metabolic processes such as digestion all dramatically slow down. This decreases the organism's need for water. When rains return, aestivating organisms become active again.

Hibernating toad

Astonishing fact

The Mascarene frog can leap to more than 17 ft in a single jump. Several frog species can leap to about 20 times their body length in one go.

Food habits

All adult amphibians are meat eaters, or carnivores. They actively search for other animals, usually insects, to eat. Adult amphibians consume a wide variety of foods. Earthworms are the main diet of burrowing caecilians, whereas anurans and salamanders feed primarily on insects and other arthropods. Large salamanders and some large anurans eat small vertebrates, including birds and mammals.

All tadpoles have special scraping mouthparts that are used for feeding on algae. Tadpoles of a few species, especially the spade foot toads, sometimes become cannibals. They often eat their fellow tadpoles and can grow to enormous size.

Amphibians generally are not very particular about what they eat. Just about anything that is alive and fits in their mouth is fair game for adult salamanders and frogs. Spiders, snails, worms, insects and crayfish are common in amphibian habitats and are eaten regularly. Narrowmouth toads are one of the few amphibians that eat mostly one thing. They specialize in eating ants.

Astonishing fact

Amphibians must shed their skin as they enlarge in size. The old skin is discarded like a piece of clothing that has become too tight. Usually the shed skin is eaten.

Means of defence

Compared to other vertebrates, which maybe faster and stronger or possess poisonous bites or sharp claws, amphibians are relatively easy prey. In water and on land, they are pursued by a hungry throng of birds, mammals, reptiles, fishes and other amphibians. Yet they have managed to survive for millions of years.

Amphibians don't have fangs and talons, but their subtle defence systems still function well. They have relatively small, slippery bodies and a generally quiet and retiring nature. Many species don't show themselves in daylight. Amphibians also have other survival tricks, many involving coloration.

Flashing

Flash coloration is different from warning coloration because it is not seen until the amphibian is under attack. The bright colours distract and confuse predators and help the amphibians escape.

Tricks

Imitating poisonous species can help keep salamanders alive. Some use the old trick of playing dead. Others protect themselves by biting. Sirens even scream and yelp. One unusual defence is the ability to survive, at least for a while, in the stomach of a predator. Poisonous Red Efts can live there up to 30 minutes, by which time they have usually been spit up by whatever swallowed them.

Astonishing fact

Frogs absorb water through their skin so they don't need to drink.

Poisons

Many amphibians produce mild skin poisons, and some secretions are toxic enough to kill predators. In salamanders, the tail is often the most poisonous part (and the part predators can most easily grab).

Colour-change artists

Changing skin colouration is employed by frogs, toads, and some salamanders. Tree frogs and other colour-change artists change their colours over time to match the background they rest upon.

Protective colouration is important to many amphibians, a large number of which are green, brown, or gray—colours that are common in nature. These colour patterns act as camouflage, helping amphibians blend in with their surroundings.

Astonishing fact

Some frogs can survive in conditions well below freezing. The Grey tree frog for example can survive even though its heart stops. It does this by making its own antifreeze which stops its body from freezing completely.

Standing out

Warning colouration is the opposite of protective colouration. Bright colours on the upper surface of the skin usually mean the amphibian has quite poisonous skin. Predators that attack a brightly coloured amphibian quickly learn to avoid similar-looking ones in the future.

Environmental significance

Amphibians play a very important role in the ecosystem. Tadpoles are the prey items for both invertebrates and vertebrates. Adult amphibians are the best biological pest controllers. Invertebrates and vertebrates also predate them. Because of their importance in ecosystem, decline or extinction of their population has significant impact on other organisms along with them.

Amphibians are highly used in medical research. Epibatidine, a skin extract from a South American frog blocks the pain 200 times more effectively than morphine. Poison dart frogs have highly toxic skin compounds that are smeared to arrows to kill larger animals.

In the last half of the twentieth century, scientists noted the alarming decline in the numbers of amphibians around the world. They theorized the decline was due to a number of factors: pollution of freshwater ecosystems, the destruction of amphibian habitats, increased ultraviolet radiation due to ozone depletion and diseases like chytridiomycosis. Amphibians are known as indicator species, or species whose health is an indicator or sign of the health of the ecosystem they inhabit. As their numbers decrease, so do the number of healthy ecosystems around the world, which in turn results in the loss of many other animal and plant species.

Astonishing fact

Research has shown that Ammonium Nitrate (a fertilizer) can cause agonizing death for frogs. Frogs suffer a massive toxic attack if they come in contact with it.

Some amphibian extremes:

- The largest amphibian in the world is the Chinese Giant Salamander reaching a length of 180 cm from the nose to the tip of the tail.
- The largest frog is the Goliath Frog. It can grow up to 13 inches in length, and weighs up to 3 kg.
- The largest caecilian is Caecilia thompsoni which reaches 151.5 cm.
- The smallest salamander is Thorius arboreus. The average length of several specimens of this salamander was only 17 mm.
- The smallest frog in the world is the Monte Iberia Eleuth; a frog only recently discovered on a mountain in Cuba. Specimens have been found that are only 8.5 mm long! It is considered Critically Endangered and is found in only 2 small areas on Cuba. Since this frog was only discovered in 1996, and only females have been found, very little is known about this tiny frog.

Some well-known amphibian

Blue Poison Dart Frog

Often said to be the most alluring of all frog species, the blue poison frog's colouration is actually thought to function as a warning to predators that it is poisonous. They have extremely poisonous skin. They have glands in the skin that produce strong toxins. Their poison is used by some South American Indians for applying to the tips of their hunting arrows and blow-gun darts.

The bright coloration of the poison frog warns predators that they are poisonous. Once a predator has even licked a poison arrow frog, it gets very sick and will never try to eat one again. The poison protects them from most predators.

Blue poison dart frogs live in tropical rainforests of South and Central America. They eat ants, termites, flies, small beetles, spiders, etc.

Blue poison dart frog

Chinese giant salamander

Chinese Giant Salamander

The Chinese giant salamander is the largest salamander in the world, and is fully aquatic. It grows up to 180 cm in length. It lives in cool, fast-flowing streams and mountain lakes and predominantly feeds on fish and crustaceans. This species is threatened by over-harvesting for the food trade, as well as the destruction and degradation of its habitat. It is now Critically Endangered, having undergone a massive population decline over the last 30 years.

Axolotl

The name 'axolotl' is thought to have originated from the Aztecs, derived from two words: atl, meaning 'water', and xolotl meaning 'monster'. This astonishing species is part of the family of 'mole salamanders', but exhibits an unusual and extreme trait known as neoteny, or paedomorphosis. Axolotls do not develop adult characteristics but retain their gills, fins and other larval characteristics throughout their life. They live permanently in water, in the wetlands and canals associated with Lake Xochimilco and Lake Chalco, adjacent to Mexico City. Once eaten as a delicacy in Mexico City, they are now a protected species in Mexico and Critically Endangered in the wild.

Axolotl

Purple frog

Purple Frog

The sole surviving member of an ancient group of amphibians that evolved some 130 million years ago, the discovery of the purple frog has been described as a 'once-in-a-century find'. The Purple Frog is a very recent discovery, having being discovered in India in 2003 making the Purple Frog the first new family of frogs to be discovered since 1926. Currently the Purple frog is listed as endangered because the growth of deforestation is destroying its habitat.

Reaching around 7 cm in length the Purple Frog has a mixed coloration of purple and gray and is somewhat bloated in appearance. The head of the Purple Frog is very small compared to its body and the same is true with its limbs. As the Purple Frog spends most of its life underground it is an expert burrower making use of growths on its hind limbs to aid in burrowing.

Budgett's Frog

The Budgett's Frog, along with its wide comical face, has a body that seems entirely too large for its legs. These characteristics have led to another common name; it is also called the 'hippo frog'. The two sharp protrusions in their mouth allow them to attack both prey and predator alike. This frog is also known as the 'Freddy Kruger' frog, because when frightened, it will open its disproportionately large mouth and emit a shrill scream.

Budgett's frog

Some well-known amphibians

Goliath Frog

The goliath frog is the largest frog in the world. Measuring up to 13 inches in length and weighing up to 3.3 kg, the goliath frog is as big as some house cats! It doesn't start out so big, though. The tadpole of the goliath frog is the same size as the tadpole of an average frog but just keeps growing.

Goliath frogs are found in small ranges in the rain forests at the equator of western Africa, near swift-moving rivers and waterfalls. These giant amphibians need to be near water much like the average frog. They come out at night and sit on river rocks to look for food. An adult goliath frog eats the same types of food that other frogs do: insects, crustaceans, fish, and other amphibians.

Goliath frog

African Giant Toad

The African giant toad is a large, forest-dwelling species, with attractive colouration that provides perfect camouflage amongst the leaf litter. The yellowish upperparts resemble a fallen leaf, and are even marked with blotches and frayed edges to imitate decay. By contrast, the under parts are dark purple-red giving the appearance of the shadow cast by the leaf.

African giant toad

19

Tomato Frog

The tomato frog is found only on the large island of Madagascar. As the name indicates, tomato frogs are tomato red with a black eye line and green eyes. The females are brighter red and larger than the males.

This bright red frog inflates itself when threatened and looks just like a ripe tomato. Its vivid coloration also serves as a warning sign to predators that it will not taste good. When attacked or handled, it secretes copious amounts of sticky mucus from its skin; any animal trying to eat it is likely to find its jaws glued together.

Common Toad

The Common Toad is also known as the European Toad. Common toads are widespread in mainland Britain, Europe, northwest Africa and Asia. Adult Common toads can grow to be 18 cm in length. The most obvious feature that distinguishes this species from frogs is its warty skin in colours ranging from olive greens to orange browns. As a defence against predators they secrete a toxic, foul tasting substance called 'bufagin' that prevents most predators from wanting to eat them.

Common toad

Tomato frog

Some well-known amphibians

Southern Gastric-brooding Frog

The gastric-brooding frogs were ground-dwelling frogs native to Queensland in eastern Australia. When the gastric brooding frog was discovered in 1973, it was abundant. The decline began in 1979. There has been no report in the wild since 1981. The reasons for the species' sudden decline are unknown.

This frog employed one of the most original life-history strategies in the animal kingdom – gastric brooding. Females would swallow their eggs and allow the young frogs to develop into tadpoles, and subsequently froglets, in her stomach. During the brooding period the female's digestive process would shut down and her stomach would become so bloated that her lungs would collapse under the pressure, forcing her to rely solely on gas exchange through her skin for respiration.

Waxy Monkey Leaf Frog

This frog is unique in many ways. This brightly coloured species of frog is commonly known as the Waxy Monkey Leaf Frog, found in Argentina, Brazil, Bolivia and Paraguay. It moves by walking rather than hopping, which is the reason for the 'monkey' in its name. It is a very calm, careful creature. It has adapted to meet the demands of life in the trees. It does not need to return to the ground during the mating season, rather it lays its eggs down the middle of a leaf before folding the leaf, sandwiching the eggs inside. Its nest is attached to a branch suspended over a stream so that hatching tadpoles drop into the water.

Southern gastric-brodding frog

Waxy monkey leaf frog

AMPHIBIANS

Darwin's frog

Darwin's Frog

Another strange frog is the Darwin's frog. It got its name after the fact that Charles Darwin discovered it on his world voyage. This frog lives in the cool forest streams of South America, mostly in Argentina and Chile.

This frog has odd brooding habits. The female lays about 30 eggs and then the male guards them for about 2 weeks. Then the male picks up all the survivors and carry around the developing young in their vocal pouch. The tadpoles develop in their baggy chin skin, feeding off their egg yolk. When they are tiny froglets (about half an inch) they hop out and swim away!

Taylor's Salamander

Taylor's salamander exhibits some highly unusual and distinct features, indicative of its evolutionary distinctiveness. For example, it appears to be specialised for life in saline (or salty) water, as the salinity of Laguna Alchichica which it inhabits is near to the maximum tolerated by most adult amphibians, and is well above that tolerable to eggs and embryos. This salamander will basically eat anything, within reason, that fits into its mouth. It typically hides below the water line under overhangs in the crater's edge of Laguna Alchichica and is found in very deep water, often more than 30m below the surface.

Taylor's salamander

Some well-known amphibians

Olm

Olm

The olm is a type of salamander that lives in deep caves where it's dark all the time. Because it spends all its time underground, this creature has no eyes and no colour in its skin. Olms are found in the underwater caves of southern European lakes and rivers. The olm is also known as the humanfish, the cave salamander or the white salamander.

This see-through creature, which lives in subterranean caves, is blind and hunts down prey using a keen sense of smell as well as sensors that can detect weak electrical fields. It can survive for ten years with no food and can live to be more than 100 years.

Argentine Horned Frog

The Argentine Horned Frog most prominent feature is its mouth, which accounts for roughly half of the animal's overall size. It is also commonly known as the Argentine Wide-mouthed Frog or Pacman Frog.

It is found from the rain forests of Argentina, Uruguay and Brazil. It is also a voracious eater and will attempt to swallow anything that moves close to its wide mouth even if it would lead to suffocation. It is most aggressive and will attack an animal way larger that itself. They are not poisonous but they are fearless. When they feel threatened they will jump toward the enemy and bite them! When hunting, they prefer to wait for their prey to come to them and will eat other frogs, lizards, mice, and large insects.

Argentine horned frog

23

AMPHIBIANS

Malagasy Rainbow Frog

The Malagasy rainbow frog is a very attractive species that has become popular in the pet trade. The Malagasy rainbow frog lives in the rocky dry forests of Madagascar's Isalo Massif, where it breeds in shallow temporary pools found in canyons. This species is well adapted to climbing in its rocky surroundings, and can even scale vertical surfaces! When threatened, this frog will inflate itself as a defence mechanism against predators.

Mallorcan Midwife Toad

This tiny amphibian is unusual in that the male carries around the eggs wrapped round his hind legs until they hatch. The species was discovered as a fossil in 1977, but was thought to be extinct until 1980, when a live adult toad was found in a remote mountainous region of northern Mallorca.

The main threats to the survival of the Mallorcan midwife toad are introduced predators and competitors (such as the viperine snake and green frog) and human recreational activities (such as rock-climbing and mountain biking), which cause disturbance and erosion. This species is found only in the Sierra de Tramuntana of northern Mallorca in the Balearic Islands, Spain.

Malagasy rainbow frog

Mallorcan midwife toad

24

Some well-known amphibians

Emperor newt

Gardiner's Seychelles Frog

The Gardiner's Seychelles frog is very tiny, growing to a maximum length of just 11 mm or smaller than your thumbnail. This species is now found only on the Seychelles islands of Mahe and Silhouette. This species is ground-dwelling and breeds on land, where it lays small clumps of eggs on moist ground. Breeding is known to occur throughout the year and the young do not hatch as tadpoles, but as froglets.

Emperor Newt

The Emperor Newt, also known as the Mandarin Newt or Mandarin Salamander, is a species of newt native to Southeast Asia. They are found in the high mountain province of Yunnan, China.

This species can grow up to 8 inches in length. It has a ridged orange head and a single orange ridge that runs along the back. This ridge is lined with two parallel rows of orange bumps.

The Emperor Newt is mainly nocturnal. The orange warts along its back are poison glands and when grabbed the tips of the ribs will squeeze out poison from the glands. Emperor newts have enough toxins to kill approximately 7500 mice.

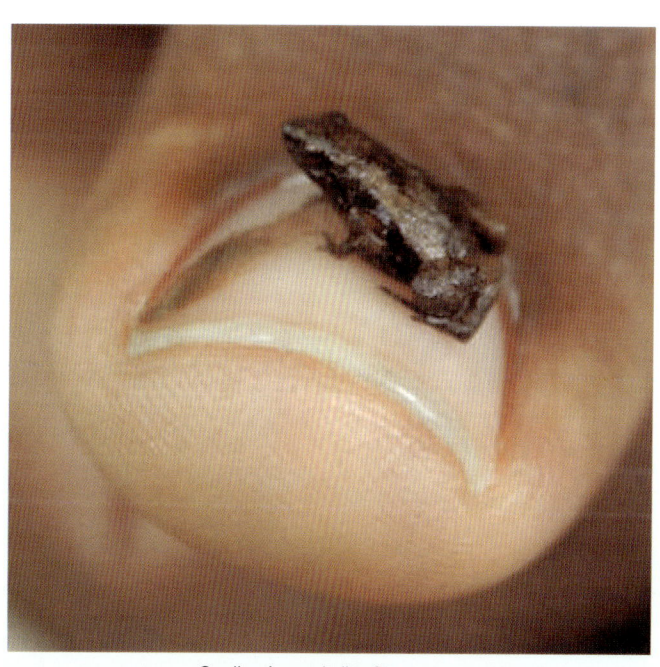

Gardiner's seychelles frog

AMPHIBIANS

Chinhai spiny newt

Chinhai Spiny Newt

The Chinhai spiny newt is a secretive, land-dwelling species that hibernates for about five months of the year during the winter. This species possesses a remarkable defence mechanism against predators. They have sharp, elongated ribs whose tips project through the skin when these animals are grasped and inject painful skin secretions into the mouths of predators. This species is only found in China.

Spotted Salamander

Named for the two rows of yellow and orange spots speckled along their black backs, spotted salamanders are large members of the mole salamander family. On average, they measure about 18 cm, but they can reach lengths up to 23 cm long!

Common in the forests of the eastern United States and eastern Canada, spotted salamanders make their homes in areas that are close to ponds and pools. But the dark amphibians are difficult to find. Adults spend most of their day hiding underground or beneath rocks and logs. Venturing out from their hiding spots at night to hunt, they eat just about anything they can catch and swallow, including worms, spiders, insects, and slugs.

When threatened, spotted salamanders secrete a mild sticky toxin from their backs and tails that dissuades predators such as skunks, raccoons, turtles, chipmunks, squirrels, opossums, and snakes from eating them.

Spotted salamander

Some well-known amphibians

Mudpuppy

Mudpuppies, also called waterdogs, are one of only a few salamanders that make noise. They get their name from the conception that their squeaky vocalizations sound like a dog's bark.

Among the largest of the salamanders, mudpuppies can exceed 41 cm in length, although the average is more like 28 cm. Their range runs from southern central Canada, through the Midwestern United States, east to North Carolina and south to Georgia and Mississippi.

Mudpuppies live on the bottoms of lakes, ponds, rivers, and streams, and never leave the water.

Mudpuppy

Solomon Island Leaf Frog

This frog is unique not only because of its notably long snout and horns but also unusual as it hatches as a perfectly formed tiny frog rather than a tadpole. It is one of the few species of frogs in the world that do this. The Solomon Island Leaf Frog lives in tropical lowland rainforests on the Solomon Islands and in Papua New Guinea.

Solomon island leaf frog

AMPHIBIANS

Pouched Frog

These frogs are an inch long, more or less, and are usually grey to red-brown in colour. The sides are dark grey to black and the belly is cream with brown spots, and there is a pink spot at the base of each arm. These frogs have no webbing, but have swollen fingers and toes.

The Pouched Frogs live in the cool, moist, mountainous Australian rainforests, and are usually found under rocks, logs, or wet leaves. These frogs are unique in that they do not need water to breed. The female lays her eggs on the ground and both she and the male stand guard. The male Pouched Frog has twin pouches, one on each side and when the tadpoles hatch, the male climbs amongst the eggs allowing the tadpoles to slide over the male's body and wriggle into the pouches where they stay until they are fully developed frogs.

Golden Toad

Last seen in 1989, this beautiful Golden Toad is now considered extinct. They were once abundant in the high altitude tropical forests of Costa Rica, but scientists believe the climate change in this area of Costa Rica have had this devastating effect on the Golden Frog population. Amphibians are extremely sensitive to climate changes that they are likened to 'a canary in a coalmine'.

Pouched frog

Golden toad

Some well-known amphibians

Cane Toad

The Cane Toad is the largest species in its family. Adult Cane Toads are usually heavy-built and weigh an average of up to 1.8kg. Their size may vary from 15-23 cm and their skin is warty. Cane toads produce powerful toxins concentrated in their glands. Under extreme stress, cane toads can release enough toxins to quickly kill a large dog. Some effects caused by its poison are burning of the eyes and hands, and skin irritation.

Oriental Fire-Bellied Toad

The Oriental Fire-bellied Toad's main feature is that their tongues do not extend like other toads or frogs. Therefore, to feed they leap forward to catch their prey in their mouths while using their forearms to stuff the prey in the rest of the way.

These toads are native to south-eastern Siberia, north-eastern China, and Korea.

Oriental fire-bellied toad

The toads have brilliantly coloured bellies which are used as warning signs that they are poisonous. The poisons are secreted onto their skin to cover the entire body. The toxins secreted by these toads can irritate or sting a human's eyes and or face. When threatened, the toads will arch their backs and display their brightly coloured bellies as a warning.

Cane toad

29

Siberian salamander

This remarkable amphibian can survive being frozen for long periods of time at temperatures of less than 35 degrees centigrade. It manages this by replacing its water with 'anti-freeze' chemicals. It's still unknown for how long they can maintain this state, but it's been documented that they can last for a few decades.

The Siberian Salamander is the only species of its kind that lives in the Arctic Circle, an environment that is totally against such organisms. Whenever facing dangerously low temperatures, it replaces the water in its body with 'anti freeze' chemicals.

Basically, after a few years, being frozen under metres of ice, if the right conditions appear, it can just thaw, get up and move along. However, the exact mechanism is totally unknown.

There are 'science legends' that Siberian salamander can survive in the frost for centuries, but so far, this has not been proven. Researchers are still looking into the mechanisms that allow it to achieve this amazing state.

The Siberian salamander is a species of salamander found in north-east Asia. It is found primarily in Siberia. There are also outlying populations in northern Kazakhstan and Mongolia. It measures from 9 to 12.5 cm in length and lays 200-250 eggs per season.

Test Your MEMORY

1. How many species of amphibians are there in the world today?

2. Write any two characteristics of amphibians.

3. Write the three categories of amphibians.

4. Name any two places where amphibians are not found.

5. Are amphibians cold-blooded?

6. What do you understand by hibernation and aestivation?

7. What do amphibians eat?

8. Name the means of defence used by amphibians.

9. Which is the largest salamander in the world?

10. Name the largest frog in the world.

11. Where is the Tomato frog found?

12. Name the frog discovered by Charles Darwin.

Index

A
aestivation 11
Anurans 3, 6, 12

B
burrowing 12, 18

C
camouflage 14, 19
cannibals 12
carnivores 12
cold-blooded 3, 10

E
endangered 16, 17, 18
evolved 4, 18
extinct 4, 24, 28
extinction 15

G
Gymnophions 4, 8

H
habitats 6, 8, 9, 10, 12, 15
hibernation 11

I
invertebrates 7, 8, 15

M
metamorphosis 3
migratory 10
moulting 5

N
nocturnal 8, 25

P
poisonous 13, 14, 16, 23, 29
predator 13, 16, 18
prey 4, 13, 15, 18, 23, 29

S
salamanders 3, 7, 8, 9, 11, 12, 13, 14, 17, 26, 27
species 3, 4, 5, 6, 7, 8, 9, 10, 11, 12, 13, 15, 16, 17, 19, 20, 21, 24, 25, 26, 27, 29, 30

T
tropical 4, 8, 9, 16, 27, 28

U
Urodeles 3, 7

V
vertebrates 3, 4, 12, 13, 15